MAR   2012

W9-CFQ-321

Instruments and Music

Strings

Daniel Nunn

Heinemann Library
Chicago, Illinois

www.heinemannraintree.com
Visit our website to find out
more information about
Heinemann-Raintree books.

To order:
☎ Phone 888-454-2279
🖥 Visit www.heinemannraintree.com
to browse our catalog and order online.

© 2012 Heinemann Library
an imprint of Capstone Global Library, LLC
Chicago, Illinois

All rights reserved. No part of this publication may be reproduced
or transmitted in any form or by any means, electronic or
mechanical, including photocopying, recording, taping, or any
information storage and retrieval system, without permission in
writing from the publisher.

Edited by Dan Nunn, Rebecca Rissman, and Sian Smith
Designed by Joanna Hinton-Malivoire
Picture research by Mica Brancic
Production by Victoria Fitzgerald
Originated by Capstone Global Library Ltd
Printed and bound in China by Leo Paper Products Ltd

15 14 13 12 11
10 9 8 7 6 5 4 3 2 1

Library of Congress Cataloging-in-Publication Data
Nunn, Daniel.
  Strings / Daniel Nunn.
      p. cm.—(Instruments and music)
  Includes bibliographical references and index.
  ISBN 978-1-4329-5062-0 (hc)—ISBN 978-1-4329-5069-9 (pb)
1. Stringed instruments—Juvenile literature. I. Title.
ML750.N86 2012
  787'.19—dc22   2010044784

Acknowledgments
We would like to thank the following for permission to reproduce
photographs: Alamy p. 13 (© Indiapicture/Phulkit Sharma); ©
Capstone Publishers pp. 21 (Karon Dubke), 22 (Karon Dubke);
Corbis p. 12 (© Todd Gipstein); Getty Images pp. 17 (Redferns/
Philip Ryalls), 19 (Digital Vision/Peter Dazeley); iStockphoto p. 7
bottom right (© DNY59); Photolibrary pp. 4 (© Image Source), 7
bottom centre (Amanaimages/Amana Productions), 8 (Mauritius /
Doug Scott), 11 (Photononstop/Bernard Foubert), 16 (Flirt Collec-
tion/Chris Rogers), 20 (Tips Italia/Hermes Images), 23 top (image-
broker.net/Peter Schickert), 23 bottom (Mauritius /Doug Scott);
Shutterstock pp. 5 (© Richard Goldberg), 6 (© Arena Creative), 7
left (© Dmitry Skutin), 7 top centre (© M E Mulder), 7 top right
(© Timmary), 9 (© Joyce Marrero), 10 (© Patrick Hermans), 14 (©
eAlisa), 15 (© VILevi), 18 (© Barone Firenze).

Cover photograph of a Mariachi Band in San Diego, California,
reproduced with permission of © Getty Images (The Image Bank/
Brett Froomer). Back cover photograph of an electric guitar
reproduced with permission of Shutterstock (© Richard Goldberg).

We would like to thank Jenny Johnson, Nancy Harris, Dee Reid,
and Diana Bentley for their assistance in the preparation of
this book.

Every effort has been made to contact copyright holders of
material reproduced in this book. Any omissions will be rectified in
subsequent printings if notice is given to the publisher.

Contents

String Instruments

guitar

drum

People play many instruments to make music.

string

A string instrument has strings
stretched across it.

People make a sound by touching
the strings.

There are many types of string instruments.

Plucking

oud

People use their fingers to play some string instruments. This is called plucking.

8

People use their fingers to play
a ukulele.

People use their fingers to play
a balalaika.

People use their fingers to play
a kora.

Using a Bow

bow

People use a bow to play other
string instruments.

People use a bow to play a sarinda.

People use a bow to play a cello.

People use a bow to play a violin.

Playing String Instruments

Some people play string instruments together.

sitar

Some people play string instruments on their own.

Some people play string instruments for work.

Some people play string instruments just for fun!

Making String Instruments

Some string instruments are hard to make.

Some string instruments are easy to make.

Play Your Own String Instrument

You can play your own string instruments, too!

Picture Glossary

 **bow** a stick with horsehairs stretched across it which is used to play some string instruments

 **plucking** pulling and letting go of strings on a musical instrument to make different sounds

Index

Notes for Parents and Teachers

Before reading

Find examples of string instruments to share with the children. Some online examples with audio can be found at: http://www.sfskids.org/templates/instorchframe.asp?pageid=3. Can they name any of the instruments? How do they think the instruments are played? Explain that some string instruments are played with a bow (such as the violin) and some are played by hand (such as the guitar). When they play by hand, people move their hands across the strings or gently pull and let go of strings (plucking). Demonstrate if possible.

After reading

Encourage the children to make their own string instrument. Stretch some elastic bands over an old plastic container. You can then pluck the "strings." The tighter the strings, the higher the sound!

Extra information

The instruments shown on page 7 are: violin (top right), balalaika (bottom right), sanshin (bottom center), electric guitar (center), and harp (left).
String instruments have higher and lower strings. This depends on how tight the strings are stretched and how thin or thick they are. High strings are normally very thin, and low strings very thick.